Heartstrings Woven in Time

A Poetry Collection

Rachika Srivastava

BookLeaf Publishing

India | USA | UK

Made with ❤ on the BookLeaf Publishing Platform
www.bookleafpub.in
www.bookleafpub.com

Dedication

To everyone who believed in my words,

*Who encouraged me, supported me, and took the
time to read what I had to say.*

*Thank you for being my motivation and my
sounding board.*

Your presence has been a guiding light.

To myself, for nurturing the passion to write,

*For giving words to thoughts and transforming
life's experiences into verses.*

And to life, for the endless inspiration,

*For the highs and lows, the quiet moments, and
the chaos.*

Each experience has shaped these poems.

Acknowledgement

A heartfelt thank you to everyone who has supported me on this journey. To my husband, Vivek, for his constant belief in me. To my family and friends, for their love and faith, and to those who embraced this poetic adventure with kindness. A special mention to my son, Avyay, whose smile fills my life with energy. This collection reflects the moments and connections that have shaped my writing. Thank you all for helping me pursue my passion and bring this vision to life.

Preface

In the quiet corners of our hearts, where love and longing reside, poetry becomes a vessel for our deepest emotions. *Heartstrings Woven In Time* emerges from those delicate, unspoken moments that shape our human experience. Each poem reflects the wide spectrum of love, from its serene beginnings to its profound revelations.

As you read, you'll traverse intimate landscapes where time dissolves, revealing the essence of shared dreams and passions.

This collection celebrates the beauty in the subtle and profound, honoring the echoes of love that resonate through every glance, sigh, and unspoken promise.

May these words mirror your own reflections and accompany your heart's journey. In these heartstrings, we weave the timeless harmony of our existence.

Love,
Rachika

Eternally Us

From the million stars that grace the sky,
You are the one who captured my eye.

The sparkle in your gaze, your tender smile,
Tugs at my heartstrings, mile by mile.

From unspoken words to whispers shared,
You built a love that none have dared.

Hand in hand, as we walk through life,
You made me feel that heaven's in sight.

Through sweet longings and playful fights,
Our bond grew stronger, day and night.

From my innocence to my moments of
madness,
You showed me love through joy and sadness.

In your embrace, I found my place,
For now I know—it's you, always.

Cosmic Love

You are the magnetic force in my life,
Lifting my soul to cosmic heights.

You are the vision that fills my eyes,
A sight I cherish, never to deny.

You are the melody of my heart's rejoice,
A dream I've chosen, my perfect voice.

You are all the colors of a rainbow combined,
Painting my world with Rembrandt's design.

Beneath the arch of your radiant hue,
I rest in the embrace of a love so true.

With you, the infinite feels so near,
A boundless love that conquers fear.

I think of You

When the stars come out to twinkle,
And the wind rustles softly through the trees,
When moonlight spills across the room,
I think of you.

When the sun's rays greet the morning,
And birds chirp, fluttering through the sky,
When the leaves sway gently in the breeze,
I think of you.

When twilight casts its golden hue,
And fireflies light up the velvet night,
When fairies dance on tiptoes unseen,
I think of you.

When the darkest hour of night descends,
And the world lies still in quiet dreams,
When the dreamland calls to restless hearts,
I think of you.

Every day,
Every hour,
Every fleeting moment,
I think of you across the miles, and love you
more.

Silent Bonds

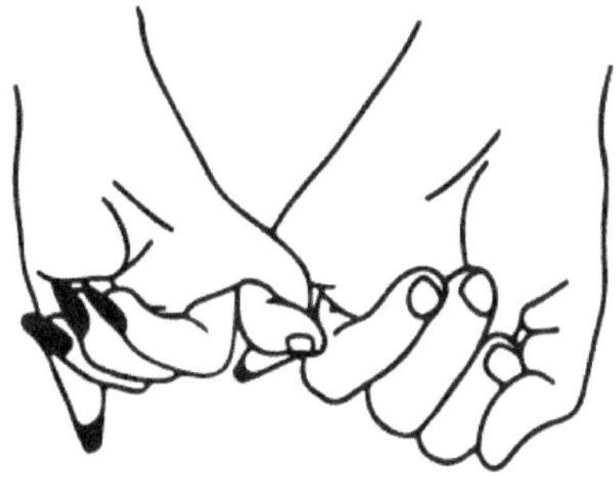

Some people enter our lives like a breeze,
With no grand reason, just a quiet ease.
Their presence sprinkles magic on the day,
Turning the ordinary to something bright and
gay.

Life feels more colorful with them around,
In their silent company, joy is found.
Yet to say it's without reason wouldn't be
true,
For the heart knows things we don't always
view.

Perhaps it's their kindness, their soul's gentle
grace,
That touches hearts in a mysterious space.
But who they impact is beyond our control,
It's God's quiet hand guiding the soul.

Not every bond needs purpose or plan,
Some are just pure, like a child's laugh or a
hand.
Naive and tender, like an innocent smile,
Simple and sweet, yet wonderfully wild.

Across the distance

I see you,
And so does he.
Though distance separates us,
You're close in spirit, eternally.

The love that links us,
Weaves through time and space,
Binding our souls in a tender embrace.

In your gentle glow,
Our hearts find solace,
A beacon of warmth in the quiet night,
A reminder that love is endless.

Whether near or far,
True love remains,
An eternal flame that never wanes,
Forever pure, through joy and pains.

Though we may be apart,
In the depths of our hearts,
The essence of love unites us,
An unbreakable bond that never departs.

Yearning for you

In shadows deep, where moonlight fades,
Desperation lingers in silent cascades.
Heartbeats echo in the night's embrace,
Longing for your presence in this empty
space.

Each breath a whisper, a plea untold,
Yearning for your touch, so pure, so bold.
In every star that twinkles above,
I see the reflections of our boundless love.

Like a flower reaching for the sun's gentle
kiss,
I ache for you in moments of bliss.
Through the vastness of time and the depths
of the sea,
I'm lost without you, longing to be free.

Let your love be my guiding light,
Illuminate my path through the darkest night.
For without you, my world's a void,
Aching, yearning to be filled and buoyed.

So hear my cries, my heart's decree,
Come back to me, and set my spirit free.
For in your arms, I find my home,
And in your love, I'm never alone.

Bound by Time, Freed by Love

Yes, I give up,
For I may never truly understand life.

The pages are closed by waves of thunder,
Yet the stories linger, making my heart
wonder.
Did I ever surrender?

Perhaps this is life—
Mysterious, wild, and untamed.
Years may pass, but no matter how I glance,
It feels like a distant ruin, lost in its own
trance.

Dragged once more into a whirlpool of
thought,
I tremble at what the future may have
brought.

Sands of time have left me adrift,
And with each passing year, I continue to lift
My gaze, still asking the same—
Did I ever surrender?

The game of hide and seek with life endures,
Its secrets veiled, a mystery so pure.
Captivating my heart, binding me tight,
In this beautiful cage, where shadows meet
light.

From ashes we came, to ashes we'll return,
Yet in love's flame, the soul will burn.
Though life's tapestry may fade in the flow,
The moments with you are all I know.

From beginning to end, I seek to understand,
This clandestine life, with its gentle hand.
The chapters may remain elusive and vast,
But your love makes each one worth the past.

Imprinted on me are the scars of time,
Yet I relive our moments in every blink of
mine.
In this endless loop, where love never dies,
I ask myself again, through heartfelt sighs—
Did I ever surrender?

A little less bright

The sun rises at its chosen hour, yet its rays
seem a little less bright.
It casts its glow across the sky, but my heart
remains untouched by its light.

The rainfall dampens the withered earth, but
fails to quench a parched soul.
Drops that should heal my barren spirit
instead slip through the cracks, leaving me
whole.

Music hums through the rhythm of life, but it
falters at the edges of my mind.
The melody drifts, unable to stir the visceral
cords that once intertwined.

The wind whistles through the towering trees,
yet its song fades into the unseen breeze.
A whisper lost, its echo dies, carried away by
the passing skies.

The stars still shimmer in the velvet night, but
their glow fails to reach my eyes.
Their distant beauty, though bright and near,
feels like a dream that disappears.

Butterflies dance above the blooming flowers,
yet the nectar remains just out of reach.
A sweetness missed, a fleeting taste, like
distant shores my heart can't embrace.

Birds gather and chirp in flocks, but their
song loses its timeless charm.
What once brought peace, now drifts away,
leaving only silence in its calm.

A little less it is, a little less it's going to be,
For all the wonders of life seem to fade—just
a little, to me.

Sojourn to life on a rainy day

As I hear the drops of rain falling on my window panes,
I walk towards the window, letting my eyes drain.

With the rain gently falling on my face,
Memories are released from time's enclosed space.

As I see the dew on the leaves,
Reawakened are dreams, stolen by time's
thief.

As the soothing wind wraps around me,
I close my eyes, drowning in an emotional sea.

Wading through the depths of this sea,
I had a long-awaited rendezvous with me.

Amazed to meet myself after so long,
I realized I'd been lost in the concepts of right
and wrong.

Understanding that desires can be
paradoxical,
I tried hard to dismiss what felt illogical.

Yet I lost the battle to my stubborn heart,
And I'm left again with the perplexed part.

As I hear the thunder roll in the cloud,
I wake from my abyssal dream, now one
among the crowd.

As the smell of wet soil rises through the air,
I'm mesmerized and surrender to life's tender
care.

With my eyes reopened, I now clearly see,
I've been blessed with a new vision to
rediscover life's beauty.

Life is beautiful, life is serene,
But to sense that, you must beckon yourself
from reality to dream.

Reality may not always be what you desire it
to be,
But when your dreams walk beside you,
There's always something ahead to strive for
and achieve.

In his presence

In the warmth of his embrace, I find my
peace,
A haven where all worries softly cease.
When I am with him, joy fills every seam,
Time swiftly dances, like a passing dream.

Moments meld into an endless embrace,
His laughter, my symphony, my sacred space.
In his eyes, I see stars that never fade,
His love, my refuge, where all fears evade.

Time slips by, unnoticed and swift,
In his presence, my soul finds its lift.
With every touch, every whispered trace,
I am whole, I am home, in this love's embrace.

Each day with him, a story unfolds,
In his arms, my heart's truth is told.
Every heartbeat echoes a sweet refrain,
In his love, I am forever sustained.

Destined Hearts

Where to start from, what to write,
When you're not around, nothing seems
bright.

I feel like a cloud with no sun in the sky,
Empty and lonely, it can only cry.

I remember the moments when your hands
were in mine,
A single glance at your eyes revealed love's
design.

The world seemed beautiful, dreams felt so
real,
Each day was a joy, a new cheer to feel.

Nothing felt tough, and fears were allayed,
Being with you was all I needed, my heart
swayed.

Destiny brought us close, then pulled us
apart,
But true love's essence can never depart.

So we meet again, exchanging knowing
glances,
Wondering why fate plays such strange
dances.

Time has shown us we were meant to be,
Destined together, as the gods had decreed.

My love is true, that's all I knew,
And so God blessed me with you—dreams do
come true.

Unspoken Harmony

In the quiet hush of twilight's embrace,
Our souls converse in a timeless space.
Words unsaid dance in the air,
A silent symphony of love laid bare.

In the morning's golden tender light,
Your laughter turns the darkness bright.
Each glance, a verse; each touch, a rhyme,
Love's true essence, both gentle and sublime.

Weaving through life's intricate threads,
Our hearts beat in rhythms, where love gently
treads.

Through trials and dreams, through joy and
tears,
We craft a tapestry of endless years.

In every sigh, in every shared glance,
We find a universe in our shared dance.
True love's language, both subtle and wise,
Speaks in the silence between our eyes.

Your presence, a calm in the storm's wild
sway,
Guides me gently through the break of day.
In the depth of your gaze, I find my home,
In love's true light, we are never alone.

So let us cherish this rare, unspoken art,
A bond that lives in the depths of the heart.
For in the realm where our spirits entwine,
True love's essence is forever enshrined.

Love's Unfading Path

Though we wander on separate roads,
And the world shifts in its endless modes,
True love, like a whisper in the breeze,
Finds a way through time's gentle seas.

Our paths may curve and drift apart,
But you linger forever in my heart.
The moments we shared, the laughter and
tears,
Remain etched deeply through the years.

In dreams, you still walk by my side,
Through the corridors where memories abide.
Though destiny charted its own course,
Love's essence endures, a powerful force.

In every sunset and starry night,
In fleeting glimpses of morning light,
I feel your presence, soft and near,
A reminder of the love we held dear.

True love doesn't fade with the end of a quest,
It lives on in echoes, eternally blessed.
So though we may not be together in form,
Our love is a shelter from any storm.

We've touched the soul's most sacred place,
A connection that time cannot erase.
For true love's journey is never in vain,
It endures beyond joy, beyond pain.

First light

In the soft glow of my earliest days,
I stumbled upon love's gentle ways.
A flutter in my chest, a sudden spark,
As if the world shifted from dark to light.

Your eyes held the promise of a new sunrise,
A clarity I'd never quite realized.
Every moment with you felt like a revelation,
Love's first light, pure and full of fascination.

Your laughter became my favorite tune,
Your touch, a warm and comforting boon.
In each shared glance, in every touch,
I learned what love could mean so much.

It was like learning a new language, so clear,
Each heartbeat, each sigh, brought it near.
In the innocence of our first embrace,
I felt a universe in your gentle grace.

So here's to the heart's first, tender find,
A love that opens both soul and mind.
In those early moments, sweet and new,
I discovered what love truly could do.

Soul's Symphony

In the quiet moments when all feels still,
I sense your presence, a calming thrill.
Our souls converse in a language so rare,
An unspoken bond floating through the air.

We connect on a level beyond the touch,
A silent understanding that says so much.
Even when we're apart, I feel you near,
A connection so deep, it's crystal clear.

It's in the way our thoughts seem to align,
When you share a glance, I know what's on
your mind.
Across miles and moments, our hearts stay
close,
In a rhythm that only true love knows.

We share a secret language that's all our own,
A whisper of feelings that have always shown.
When the world's noise tries to pull us away,
I find comfort in knowing you're just a
thought away.

Soulmates, we navigate life's winding road,
With a bond so strong, it lightens the load.
In dreams, we meet, and our hearts converse,
A telepathic love that's simple and terse.

So here's to the souls who find their match,
In a world where true love is more than a
catch.
We're woven together in a dance so sweet,
In the symphony of love, our hearts beat.

Unyielding Flame

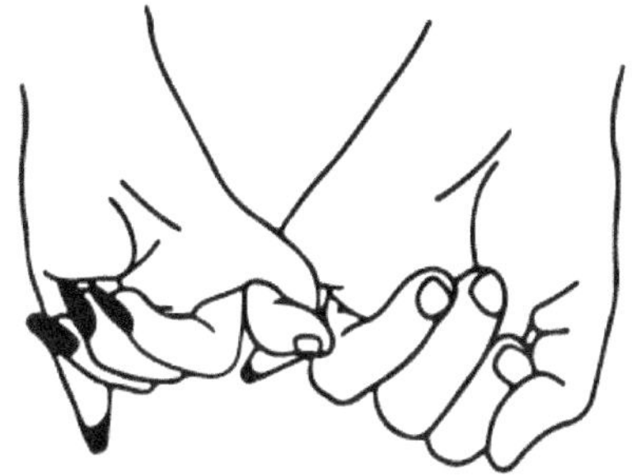

When life throws storms and wild winds our
way,
Our love stays strong, come what may.
It's the steady hand that holds me tight,
A beacon guiding us through the night.

When the world seems determined to shake
us apart,
I find comfort in your open heart.
Together we face every bump and bend,
Our love's strength is our truest friend.

In quiet moments of shared smiles and tears,
We tackle our fears, allaying doubts and fears.
Our connection is a refuge, safe and real,
A testament to the way we feel.

Through the darkest nights and brightest
days,
Our love remains, never losing its blaze.
It's a warm flame that lights our way,
Guiding us gently through each new day.

Hand in hand, we face life's twists and turns,
In each challenge, our passion burns.
With you by my side, every trial feels right,
True love's strength is our guiding light.

So here's to the love that doesn't fade,
To the bond we've built, never to trade.
Against all odds and through every high and
low,
True love's strength is all we need to know.

Nature's Love Song

Love flows like a river, winding and free,
Carving its path through the heart of the sea.
It starts from a spring, pure and bright,
Nurtured by dreams and tender light.

Mountains stand tall, steadfast and grand,
Their peaks touch the sky, strong and
unmanned.
In their shadows, love finds its space,
A constant presence, a sacred place.

Rivers may meander, bend, and twist,
But their journey is marked by love's gentle
mist.

Through valleys deep and meadows wide,
Love travels on with an unbreakable stride.

Mountains wear time's marks, weathered and
wise,
Their strength mirrored in love's tender ties.
Even in storms and shifting winds,
Love remains as steady as the peaks and crags.

Forests embrace the rivers with grace,
Their leaves whisper secrets in a soft embrace.
Nature's dance is a rhythm divine,
Reflecting the love that's yours and mine.

As rivers merge with the endless sea,
Love blends into eternity.
Through every mountain, every flowing
stream,
Our hearts find their place in a timeless
dream.

So here's to love, a force so grand,
Flowing through life, hand in hand.
In the grandeur of nature's endless show,
Love's eternal flow continues to grow.

Venus Embrace

Under the soft glow of Venus' gentle light,
Our love unfolds in the quiet of the night.
Like the planet's tender shine up above,
Our hearts mirror the warmth of our love.

We wander through life, hand in hand,
Finding our way in this vast, wondrous land.
Your touch feels like a whisper from the stars,
A reminder of how love heals and how it
spars.

In your eyes, I see the sparkle of the evening
sky,
A reflection of Venus, where our dreams lie.
Every kiss we share feels like a promise true,
Our love, timeless, in a world made for just us
two.

When we're together, the world seems to
align,
Guided by Venus, our hearts intertwine.
So here's to the love that lights our way,
In the embrace of Venus, come what may.

With you by my side, every moment feels
right,
As if Venus herself is blessing our night.
Our love is a journey, a celestial dance,
In the glow of Venus, we've found our
romance.

Whispers Through the Void

In the stillness of the night, I send my plea,
Hoping my whispers reach where you might
be.

Every tear I shed, every heartfelt sigh,
Is a love letter carried through the evening
sky.

Though distance separates our worlds apart,
I imagine my feelings finding your heart.

In dreams, I hope our souls touch and
entwine,
With my cries of longing crossing space and
time.

The nights are long, and the silence deep,
Yet my love echoes through the void I keep.

Feel my warmth in the stars' soft glow,
Knowing my heart's messages always flow.

Though we're apart, my love remains near,
In every beat of my heart, you're always here.

My Heart's Reflection

You're the calm in my chaotic day,
The soothing touch that guides my way.
Every time you smile, my heart's in flight,
You turn the ordinary into pure delight.

Your laughter is a melody I adore,
A tune that brightens my days more and
more.
Your touch is a comfort, gentle and true,
A reminder of how deeply I cherish you.

You're the light that dispels the dark of night,
The warmth that makes everything feel right.
When I gaze into your eyes, so kind and
bright,
I see the love that makes my heart take flight.

Your words are soft, like a tender embrace,
They calm my fears and bring a smile to my
face.
In those quiet moments, so serene and still,
I find peace and love, a perfect thrill.

You're the joy that turns my sorrow to cheer,
The one who makes everything feel clear.
With you, each day is a cherished gift,
Filled with a love that gives my heart a lift.

So here's to you, my heart's true guide,
The one who makes my world open wide.
You mean more than words can convey,
You're my heart's home, now and always.

Timeless Radiance

Under the starlit sky, where dreams take
flight,
Our love shines like an endless, tender light.
It flows through the ages, never fading away,
A constant warmth that brightens each day.

As time weaves its intricate, endless dance,
Our hearts remain close, given every chance.
Each beat and breath is a promise we make,
A love that endures through each heartache.

Our connection feels like a whisper in the
night,
A soft melody that turns darkness to light.
With every sunrise and moonbeam's glow,
I feel your love, wherever I go.

Through the pages of our lives and each
shared kiss,
We craft a story filled with endless bliss.
In every glance and every touch so sweet,
We find a love that's complete and replete.

So here's to our bond that defies the years,
A love strong enough to conquer all fears.
In the dance of life and time's endless sea,
Our love is timeless, as deep as it can be.